S0-AXK-141

To:

_____

From:

_____

NOTES TO MY DAUGHTER

Before You Go

Vesna M. Bailey

OMNI Publishing
Leamington, Ontario, Canada

Dedication

For Lauren and Karyn,
my rainbows to keep.

Contents

Go confidently in the
direction of your dreams.
Live the life you've imagined.

~ Henry David Thoreau

Introduction

Once upon a dream enchanted every mother saw her daughter's name ablaze with a radiance beyond compare… and without our daughters, a certain love story would never have been told.

I wrote this book for my own daughter, Lauren, when she was leaving home to go away to university, to explore and pursue her own enchanted dreams for a fantastic journey ahead, all of her own.

In the gift and privilege of loving our daughters we tried our best to protect them, to reassure them of life's goodness and all its promises, to enable them to be independent and open minded, to empower them to be strong and loving, to challenge them to be nobly vulnerable to reflect in themselves the best of humanity, and to always search for the best of humanity in others, and the world around them.

So… what would we say to our daughters at this time when they bravely leave their childhood behind? What a fantastic dream to be realized lays ahead of them! Our window of opportunity suddenly seems so small – yet there are so many things we want to remind them of… just one more time, before they go out the door.

Yes, we want to say: Today is your moment in time – carpe diem (seize the day)! Run out this door with all the joy, exuberance, passion, and energy that you can muster. Know that the decisions and choices you make, your words and deeds – they will be the thumbprint you leave on the world. You have an obligation to yourself, to find a peace and happiness, and you have an obligation to your fellow man, to care… and to act accordingly.

From now on you are the weaver of your own tapestry, and that is as it should be. Challenge yourself to rise beyond the limits you once thought impossible and you will soar to heights untold.

…as for me, I am not going anywhere. I will always be there to write your name in the sand each time the tide washes it away. I will be there to applaud you when all the other chairs are empty. I will be there to catch your dreams… to love you, always and forever.

Thank-you for letting me journey with you thus far; it has been a privilege beyond compare. You are a little piece of heaven that fills my every breath… you are my rainbow to keep.

Now, gallop away into the new horizons awaiting you… my eyes will always be watching you… never will I lose sight of you!

Catch me a rainbow,
a rainbow to keep,
so I can dream pretty colored dreams,
and with gladness awaken and breathe,
so I can dine with kings and queens,
and with paupers and shepherds,
so I can yell out, in a voice of every color,
"Just you wait and see all that I can be,
all that I will be,
just you wait and see,
don't take your eyes off of me!"

~ Mom

Carpe diem. (Seize the day)

~ Horace (65 – 8 BC)

A STANDING OVATION

One enchanted day, like no other,
a star, like no other, was born,
and that was you.

Love yourself. Believe in yourself.
You are amazing!
Bright, caring, loving, fair, genuine, funny, insightful, level headed,
focused, unique, graceful, elegant, and… beautiful,
inside and out!

Sculpt a concept of spirituality that you are comfortable with and
abide accordingly through living a good, honest, joyful, and kind life.

Live an uncommon life –
chase an uncommon happiness.

Do it.
Be it.
Live it.
Now!

~ Mom

Be yourself.

Be proud.

Care.
Be kind, sensitive, compassionate and generous.

Be genuine.

Love.

Laugh.

Get excited! Dream it! Live it!

Live like you mean it — with passion and fortitude.

ALL AWHIRL! ... CATCH ME If You Can...!

Do not quiet the whispers from your heart and soul –
Turn up the volume,
Let your spirit soar,
Let your imagination fly,
Let your laughter sing,
Let your footsteps chase your inspirations, and
Let your life live.
~ Mom

Give away your smile! A million times a day!

Do not wish your life away. Chase your own dream!
Live your own dream!
Begin now.

Make your favorite story the one you are living in right now.

Just trust yourself,
Then you will know
How to live.

~ Johann Wolfgang von Goethe

Don't hold your breath – life moves along at lightning speed.

If you recognize that every moment, in its own way,
is uncommonly precious, you will gather extraordinary riches
over your lifetime.

As they say, life is not a dress rehearsal.
We cannot go back and say the things we didn't then say,
do the things we didn't then do, or live the life we didn't then live.
Grasp for your own truths on time.

Burst anew into your day, the morning glory of a new horizon!
Know that that day, something will happen, something will be,
that will make that day like no other.
Maybe you will hear all the colors of the wind!

Be a girl!
Step into life, on a moonlit night, with your slippers of glass.
Wear your tiara, fill your heart with laughter, imagine that
midnight will never strike.
Yes! Why not?!

Make a date with yourself once in a while.
Do exactly what you want to do! Whatever!!!

Treat yourself now and then – you deserve it!

Make up a list of at least ten things you want to do in your lifetime
at least once.

Raise a toast to good times, always!

Roller skate until you are 90! – if only in your imagination!

Don't "plan" everything!

Act on your inspirations when they occur.
With time, the moment fades and the magic is forever lost.

Nothing great was ever achieved
without enthusiasm.

~ Ralph Waldo Emerson

Create.
It doesn't matter what.
Your hands are the vessels by which hidden treasures will emerge.

Walk with a spring in your step, a twinkle in your eye,
a smile within your heart, a vision within your grasp.
Let it show!

Dream!
Build sand castles in the sky!

Give "tight" hugs.

Give firm handshakes.

Stand up straight.

Treat yourself to nice perfume.

Cheer loudly.
Clap passionately.

Drink good wine.

Tip well.

Learn how to waltz.

Things and people are
Beautiful if you love them.

~ Jean Anouilh

Don't be short on flowers in your life.
Give them freely and often.

SUNFLOWERS

Always TURN TO THE SUN

As they say, in truth life is like a box of chocolates –
you never know what you are going to get.
React carefully, choose wisely, handle setbacks gracefully,
and stay excited about the limitless possibilities –
forge ahead confidently.

There is nothing mystical about achieving a full and happy life –
find your purpose; live a kind, honest and good life;
be productive, creative, self-sufficient;
be open to love and being loved.

To find your purpose in life is not always easy –
be patient as you allow it to change and evolve.
Time will transform it to its intended form. Trust.

Excellence is to do a common thing
in an uncommon way.

~ Booker Taliaferio Washington

What will be your legacy? Live a life that mirrors your potential.

Dare to stand alone.

Life is the simplest of math equations —
what you put in is what you get out, in every aspect of your life.

Honor your principles always.

Know who and what you value. Honor who and what you value.

Live your life with integrity and never risk losing self-respect.

Set your standards high —
if you do not gauge them high for yourself, no one else will.

Know where you came from. At the crossroads, that knowledge will
help point you in the direction you need to go.

To err is human, to forgive, divine.

~ Alexander Pope

Be your own best friend. Let mistakes and regrets lead not only to a lesson learned but also self-forgiveness.

Gentle is the wind that brings songs of praise but ferocious is the storm that comes to question us. Trust that all things considered you did your best, and peace is yours to keep.

I disapprove of what you say,
but I will fight to the death
your right to say it.

~ Voltaire

How will the success of your life be measured?
Only your answer counts.

Respect your fellow man –
their views, challenges, perspectives, upbringing, weaknesses
and vulnerabilities, strengths and virtues.

Tolerate the different, the difficult, and the unpleasant in
the world as much as you can. Be patient.

Look deeply into people's eyes –
every fiber of their being is there like a chapter for all the
world to read. Tune in!

Try not to become bitter with the world –
know that for every cruel atrocity we hear of on the
morning news, somewhere, somehow, someone's life is
bearing witness to life's goodness.

Life is full of little miracles –
take time to notice them, to find them.
Pay homage to them. You are a miracle!

Allow yourself the time and space to admire and savor the
gifts around you – a sunset, a deed, a piece of art, a friend's
trait, someone's talent, an animal's instinct.

All things considered, time unfolds as it ultimately must.
Safeguard your conviction that life is good.

Know that time itself is the only true commodity in life –
invest all that you can! Do not waste it.

Try not to waste time on negative thoughts and energy –
be generous to understand, forgive, accept, and move on.
What have you learned?

The most wasted of all days
is that on which one has not laughed.
~ Nicholas Chamfort

When you wake up in the morning, expect it will be a great day –
amazingly it works most of the time!

Stay aware of things in your life to be thankful for.

Smile a lot – help light up the world!
Only good things can come of it.

Each day try to give at least one other person
a reason to smile, from ear to ear.

Revel in the simple pleasures of life;
not everything has to be exotic and expensive.

Live freely but responsibly.

Balance is the key to everything.

Show someone you believe in them – every day if you can.

Keep track of yourself –
once each year jot down the highlights of your year;
things you have accomplished, learned, done,
and the new dreams that have been awakened within you,
and because of you.

Wherever you go, whether it be across the globe or
across the street, notice how the love in a mother's arms
knows no skin color;
the walls of a home know of the same joys and sorrows
no matter where they stand, and the symbols of worship
echo the same promises.
We all belong. We all fit.
The sunflower turns to the same sun
no matter where it grows.

A RAINBOW TO KEEP

Attitude and gratitude –
It frees us up,
To love living,
To be happy.
~ Mom

One of life's secrets seems to lie in having the right attitude and living with a sense of unselective gratitude.

Yes, there may always be someone prettier than you, someone smarter than you, someone wealthier than you, someone skinnier than you, someone more anything than you, but no one will be a more magnificent package than you! – and when you come to truly believe that, no one will be luckier than you, and more at peace than you. Accept yourself and love yourself.

To be what we are, and
To become what we are
Capable of becoming is the
Only end of life.

~ *Robert Louis Stevenson*

Reflect upon every year as an evolution –
celebrate how you have evolved, how glorious
and unique you are!

It is gracious to adore and admire someone else, but do not
cheat yourself out of being you –
use it only to inspire the best in you.

Beware of the temptation to believe that the grass is
greener on the other side. No one has a totally charmed life,
we all pay our dues somewhere along the way –
and that is what gives our lives wealth and depth.

You will come to see that despite all planning and calculating
life seems to take on a heartbeat of its' own.
Sometimes it's time to fasten your seatbelt,
and sometimes to run footloose and fancy free.
Splish splash through the puddles!

In the middle of difficulty
lies opportunity.

~ Albert Einstein

The truth is that the best things in life are not things —
they are the moments when a dance is borne, when your
heart skips a beat —
on hearing a horse's neigh, a toddler's giggle, on smelling
freshly baked cookies, on returning a stranger's smile,
on falling asleep under a cozy blanket your grandmother
made for you…

Know that to be simultaneously strong and vulnerable are not incompatible concepts.
When you come to know that,
you will also know that you are only human,
and you will give yourself a freedom to be human.

Know when to call it a day.
Perseverance and determination is one thing but futility
is another. Walking away also sometimes requires courage,
determination, and perseverance…
and wisdom. Think it through!

Even in the night, the moon can get big and bright.
Know that what you do not have the opportunity to do in the sunlight you can tend to in the moonlight.
Some things just take a little longer, require a little more patience.

All things are difficult before
they are easy.

~ Thomas Fuller

Believe this, often the things we do not want to hear the most
are the things we need to be listening to the most.

Remember, if you have done your best you haven't failed.
And the next time, when you do succeed, celebrate!
Dance in the rain, bask in the moonlight, sleep in the shade,
let your pride echo beyond the clouds.

When all is well and good it is easy to be bright and positive –
but when the curtain falls down on us, then it is not easy, at all.
But we must try our dancing slippers in the rain, and trust that
the glimpse of moonlight in the night will soon give way,
once again, to sunlight – just like every other time.

A man is happy so long as
he chooses to be happy.

~ Alexander Solzhenitsyn

So much of life is about trust. Even when our trust is so often tested,
dreams are broken, promises so often are not kept,
still we must trust that the next time will be 'for keeps'.
That is what strength and courage are made of.

If we never had to feel the mist, or peer through a haze,
we would never know when the sun is shining on us bright.
In that way, life is gracious.

How wonderful that things do not always turn out as planned! –
sometimes we 'luck into' unexpected detours, only to later discover
life has granted us yet another gift.
It is on the detours that life happens –
it seems that is where life waits for us, with all its' sweetness,
with all its' challenges, and in the end, with all its' rewards.
Even bumpy roads eventually emerge onto level ground.

Detours are merely opportunities.
Seize the opportunity when you have it –
life has a knack of not repeating itself in this regard.

Things may not be forever, but the journey is forever.
In the end you will emerge a refined, polished, cultured pearl.
Stay the course.

Keep things in perspective.
To be hungry is not the same as to be famished.

Try not to be moody.

Don't complain and whine. Some things just have to be done,
and yes!, it's you that has to do it – so just do it!
Don't dwell on misery. Is it fair? Probably not. So what?!

Before you voice a problem or complain, work on a solution.

It may sound selfish but it is not… take care of yourself first.
It is only then that you will be able to function at your best
and do all that is required of you for others.

Trust in life. It follows its own rhythm and timing,
following due course. Some things we cannot change, but we
can trust, and must trust, that in the end it will all be alright.

You will have many "Aha!" moments where you will recognize,
"Once again, I've now come of age!"
That is the beauty of journeying –
traveling and adjusting, as needed.

Remember, everything worthwhile requires attention and
tending to – think carefully how you allot your resources of
time and energy.

As a woman, life will demand that you try on many hats.
A keen sense of timing and balance will be your challenge in
striving for a happy and full life. When it feels like a sacrifice,
think carefully whether it is worth it or not.

We must accept finite disappointment,
but we must never lose infinite hope.

~ Martin Luther King

Remember this, life does not come in black and white.
There are no clear rules.
We all try and do the best that we can, and hopefully
that will be good enough most of the time.

IT'S EVERYBODY'S BUSINESS

Begin each day with an anewed sense of awe,
That the sun has risen,
That the tree bears fruit,
That the river flows swift,
And you will come face to face with a joy for life –
That knows no end.
For it is in continually recognizing
The miracle in things seemingly ordinary
That elevates us to the only platform
From where life can cast its most magical of spells.

~ Mom

I know of only one duty,
and that is to love.

~ Albert Camus

Remember the underprivileged.

Sponsor a child in a Third World country.

Donate to charity.

At Christmas time visit one lonely person.

Donate a food basket to someone in need.

The worst sin towards our
fellow creatures is not to hate them,
but to be indifferent to them;
That's the essence of inhumanity.

– George Bernard Shaw

When you toss your coins into the cup of a homeless person,
address them by "Sir" or "Madam" –
and you will have given them a brief moment of dignity on
their weary journey.

True compassion knows no social class, no race, no ethnicity.
Be a living witness to this conviction whenever you are
entrusted with the opportunity.
Know that you were chosen for this deed.

Be aware of what is going on in the world.
Try to fit it into the big picture of what you already know.
Make it a goal to learn more when you have time.

Catch the daily news highlights.
Try to flip through at least the Saturday edition of a good newspaper;
be aware of the world around you.

What will survive of us is love.

~ Phillip Harkin

Help an elderly person plant a garden, offer a ride,
invite them for a visit.

Remind yourself often that the aged were once young
and vibrant too, bursting with dreams, vision and hope,
bravery and sacrifices, laughter and mischief.
Their earned wisdom which they now offer to you
is a treasure and a privilege.

There is no greater gift you can offer to an elderly, lonely
person than to lend them a bit of your time and your ear.
To feel old, spent and easily discarded is a cruel place.

If you don't stand for something...
you'll fall for anything.

~ Anonymous

Savor the opportunity to spend time with
and learn from an interesting person.

In conversations, listen and participate.
Honor the other person by showing interest in or familiarity
with the subject matter.

Vote. Make yourself heard. Know what you stand for.

Do not litter or pollute.
Recycle. Respect the earth and everything that lives therein.

Contribute to the protection of endangered plant and
animal species.

If you educate a man you educate a person,
But if you educate a woman you educate a family.
~ Ruby Manikan

MORNING BELLS

To wonder is to feed a hunger,
To discover is to grow a passion,
To use your knowledge is to live with a reason.
~ Mom

Life is an adventure in learning –
discover it, live it, savor it, love it.

Strive for knowledge – it truly is powerful and invigorating.
It is the breath of life.

No bird soars too high
if he soars with his own wings.

– William Blake

Strive to complete your post-secondary education.
It will allow you to know that you can always stand on
your own two feet.
There is nothing else that will so easily lead you to feeling
self-sufficient, liberated, independent and powerful.

Remember, your knowledge is something no one can ever
take away from you.

Use your knowledge to serve and to benefit others
whenever you are entrusted with the opportunity.

Our aspirations are our possibilities.

— Samuel Johnson

Never lose your sense of wonder.
Nurture it, each and every day.

To wonder is to feed a hunger, to discover is to grow a passion.
When you use your knowledge fully and responsibly
you will be living with a reason.

Once in a while gaze up at the clouds –
surely you will discover fairies and dragons, pyramids and oceans;
it's all up to you to see it.
The canvas is always there – you just have to pick up the paintbrush.

Remember, not everything worth learning has to be
immediately useful and applicable.
All knowledge has some hidden worth. It's all good!

Read! Even ten minutes a day.

Keep books all around you.
Turn the television off once in a while and flip through a book.

Over time, create your own library.
Undoubtedly it will become one of your most loved possessions.

Include books by foreign authors.

Include photography books.

Include art books.

Own the best dictionary you can afford.

They can because
they think they can.

~ Virgil

Force yourself to learn at least a bit about the classics –
literature, art, music, philosophy, mythology.
Give yourself a basic education in the liberal arts.

Acquire a good grasp on basic world history.
Lose yourself in civilizations past, in nations past,
in the trials and the glory of times past.

Branch out – read a good variety of things.
Allow yourself to develop familiarity with a broad range
of topics – life for you will then be that much more
interesting and invigorating.
You will find many more people and places interesting.
And you will be that much more interesting.

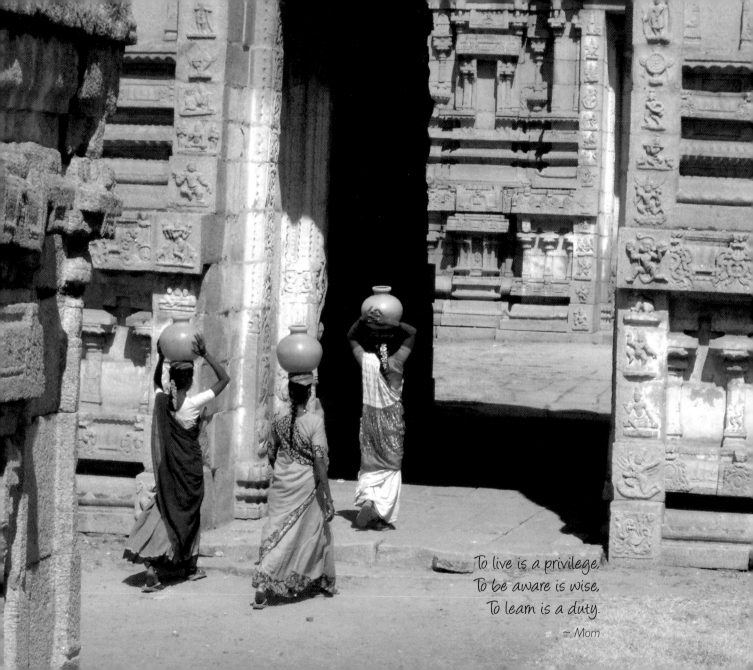

To live is a privilege,
To be aware is wise,
To learn is a duty.
~ Mom

Read autobiographies/biographies of the people that have
left their mark on the world –
in sports, social movements, history, entertainment, religion,
science, the humanities, your personal heroes, etc.

Through books you can travel the universe and get
to know the most intricate threads of the tapestry of
mankind while uncovering more pieces of your own being.
It is all connected – we are all connected.

Knowing your destination
is half the journey.

~ Anonymous

Try to learn one new word every day. It is actually hard not to!

Recognize how fortunate you are to have access to an education.
Be gracious when you meet those who might not have been
so lucky.

Force yourself if you have to, but visit an art gallery/museum and
go to a symphony at least once each year.
Listen to classical music at least once in a while –
even if it is only ten minutes a month. In time, you will come to
appreciate it more and more.

To be in pursuit of happiness...
It is as noble a calling as any.

~ Mom

Get even more familiar with the physical world – look at an atlas once in a while and try to find five new countries, islands, mountains, rivers. Imagine the worlds at your fingertips.

Travel the world as much as you can.

Keep a list of things you would like to learn more about one day, when you have time.

Learn a new language – or just try!

Rent foreign movies.

Life is wonderful! It truly is full of wonders,
but the most amazing wonders of the world
are those that lie within your own world.
There is no greater fortune
than being lucky enough to recognize them on time.

DO RE MI ...

For our life
we are accountable
first and foremost to ourselves.
Set your standards high,
keep your standards high.
Know that surely there will come a day
when you will have to reconcile with yourself.
~ Mom

Recognize your potential,
with all your gifts and all life's possibilities.

Reconcile with your responsibility to yourself to grasp
for the best within you.

Put an effort into everything you do; it shows if you do
and if you do not. Put a deserving effort into living.

Have a life plan. Keep a focus on your goals.
Recognize distractions and your vulnerabilities.

Strive for self-discipline.

Do not procrastinate – get it done!
You will sleep better and you will not have to fall
into panic mode or chaos management.

Do not get behind.
Sometimes it is impossible to catch up.

Go to bed on time.

When you are overly tired or hungry – eat and sleep.
Don't be miserable and take it out on others.

Force yourself to work early in the day.
You will be more productive and you will accomplish more.

The difference between ordinary and extraordinary,
is that little extra.

~ Anonymous

Delegate when it makes sense.
Don't carry the world on your shoulders.

Be organized.
Use labels, files, filing cabinets.
The initial time and energy you invest will be well worth the effort
when you have to find something in a hurry.

Excuses have many uses, but none that will serve you well.

Honor your integrity.

Celebrate and acknowledge the small steps as you climb them.
Keep the end in sight – and the beginning.

Live within your means.

Budget.
Allot for gifts, entertainment, travel, living expenses, and rainy days.
Invest wisely.
If it sounds too good to be true, too fast and easy, it probably is.

An ounce of spontaneity is the spice of life.
Strive for a balance between being purpose driven
and 'falling for the moment'.

ECLIPSE OF THE MOON

Tell me about strength and courage...
It is to believe after broken dreams,
It is to trust after broken promises,
It is to smile after past hurts,
It is to love after broken hearts,
It is to live as though the sunrise is imminent.
~ Mom

Count your blessings regularly.

Life is not always easy, but it is good.
Don't let go of that.

The highest reward for man's toil
is not what he gets for it
but what he becomes by it.

~ John Ruskin

Accept that some losses are necessary.

Accept that some changes are inevitable, and in the end good.

When you are feeling most vulnerable
remember your family that loves you,
your friends that cherish you,
your achievements that speak of you,
your uniqueness that defines you,
and the universe that embraces you.
Then go be of service to someone else.
Your doubts will be put to sleep.

When things seem overwhelming be thankful that you are alive,
healthy and competent enough to be given
the opportunity of this challenge –
and know it is only temporary.

Yes! In the face of adversity know that somewhere in time
your star will shine bright again.

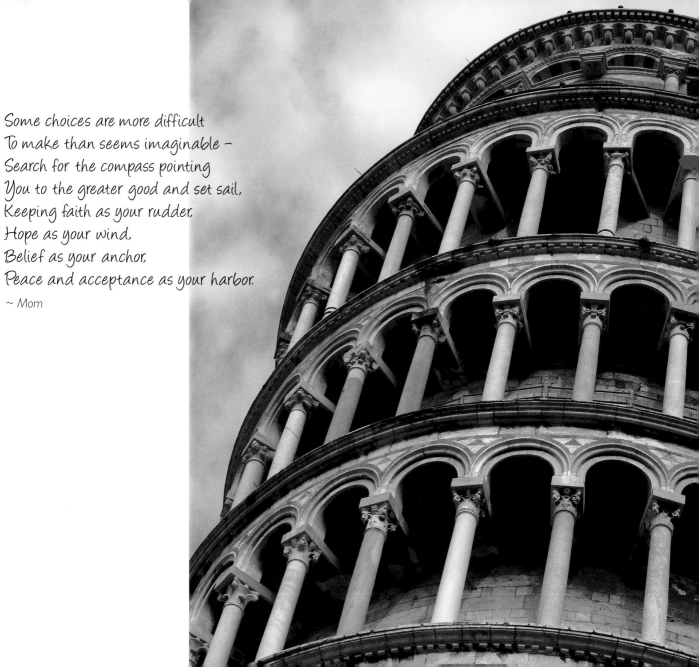

Some choices are more difficult
To make than seems imaginable –
Search for the compass pointing
You to the greater good and set sail,
Keeping faith as your rudder,
Hope as your wind,
Belief as your anchor,
Peace and acceptance as your harbor.

~ Mom

Know that self-doubt is only a glorious invitation to accept
the challenge. Conquering it transforms you and lifts you,
to once seemingly impossible heights.

Know it is OK to be scared sometimes.
It only means you have a healthy respect for,
and a healthy perspective on the situation at hand.

There is nothing heroic or intelligent
about being afraid to ask for help.
We are all smart and strong
but there are times when we all need help.

Remember, sand castles fall down
only to give us an opportunity to practice building new ones.
Realize that they are not half-fallen down,
but even with only one grain of sand remaining,
they are left half-standing and already half-built.

In the midst of winter, I finally learned
that there was in me an invincible summer.

~ Albert Camus

Know that whenever a door closes,
it will lead to a new door opening in due time.
This is only an opportunity for you to prepare for
your grand entrance.
Be patient.

Don't begrudge the painful or difficult times in your life;
this is when you were doing some of your best growing
and you were becoming the person that you are.
Challenges give us strength, validate our character,
attest to our capacity to learn,
and affirm the love and support around us.

Do not feel sorry for yourself for too long.
Look around – there are so many who would
readily trade places with you.

Do not be quick to blame others. Look within first.
You will be surprised how often it is ourselves
who are to be held accountable.
This is just another generous opportunity for us to
learn and grow.

Only she who says she did not choose,
is the loser in the end.

~ Adrienne Rich

If you strongly dislike your job, course of study, etc. – change it!
Even if it requires more education, training, or a cut in pay.
If you don't, you will be miserable,
and you will make those around you miserable.

Always keep the power to make choices.

Think long term when you consider all your options.

Laugh and cry without shame.
To feel is to be alive and bears witness to humanity.

CALL ME...

As an organ has a thousand pipes to make its sound,
so a life has thousands of journey crossings to make its way,
to later echo of the ebb and flow of life's tides,
the moments of surrender,
and the moments of triumph.

~ Mom

The best parts of the journey are the crossings —
where our paths cross with those traveled by others.
That is the only journey to take.

You will stop in many houses along the journey.
And you will have many visitors to your home…
throw away the key and keep an open heart.

Listen with your heart,
Feel with your eyes,
Do with your soul.
~ Mom

Friends are wonderful for they serve for us to self-reflect upon,
clarify and define ourselves, and we do the same for them
in return.

As it has been said before, this place where you now find yourself,
it is not a place where you have arrived alone,
it is not a place where you can stand alone.
The simple truth is that we need each other in our lives,
to journey together.
Remember this – in good times and in bad,
and honor your fellow travelers.

Our friends carry us
when our own wings forget how to fly.

Flowers are rooted and grow in soil, friendships in the shared
joys and sorrows. Tend to your garden without fail.

Share your burdens, do not keep them all to yourself –
and when called upon, help carry someone else's load.
Perhaps because of you, in time they will find strength to
carry on again.

Try not to get petty with your girlfriends.
Love them for their great qualities and ignore the rest.

Having your own thoughts and opinions is important,
and often it is imperative to make them known, but almost
just as often it is not necessary to force them onto others.

Do not close doors. Do not burn bridges.
The tides of life ebb and flow and surely you will hear a
knock on that door once again.

Fight for your dignity – and do not ever play a part in taking away someone else's dignity.

Life may at some time grant you the privilege to have some form of power –
but remember, no glory lies in having power in and of itself.
The glory lies in seeking out harmony,
a symphony borne of gives and takes, the compromises,
the seam allowances you choose to leave in order to accommodate that which is required. Be gracious.

Never extinguish someone's spirit with your position of power, and never let anyone else extinguish your spirit solely because they are temporarily in a position of power.

Some things are almost effortless, yet timeless.
The memory of a gentle kiss, a tight hug, the squeeze of a hand,
a smile, a wink…
they transport and elevate us beyond imagination.
Be generous.

Even if it is against your nature, learn to communicate.
Say it! Otherwise so much of life will pass you by, unspoken,
and unheard.

Do not be quick to judge others.
Everyone has his or her own story to tell.

Look for the good in people.
Do not expect perfection.
Choose to forgive trespasses. It is not always easy to do that
but it is often necessary.
Ultimately it is the only road that leads to
finding peace within you.

Honor those around you by showing respect through your
choice of words and actions. Know your boundaries.

Remember, self-respect and respect from others is
something that has to be earned.
One might say we are always at work in this regard.

Love is unconditional but respect is earned. It is a lot easier
never to lose the respect of others than it is to earn it back.

Give and take in all your personal and business
relationships. It's about winning at life –
not about the competition or argument.
Be aware of your motives.

Be willing to compromise, as long as it does not involve
sacrificing your values and integrity.

Work hard at listening. Ninety percent of a relationship is
determined by how well you hear.

Choose well who to discuss politics and religion with.
Don't be tempted to convince.
Be prepared to accept that others are entitled to,
and maybe even justified in, having a differing opinion
from your own.
Even in disagreement you must still maintain respect.

Consider your friendships sacred. Nurture them and cherish them.
Acknowledge and recognize the blessing of each person
in your life.

Cradle and protect the confidences entrusted to you –
as long as in doing so, no harm will come to anyone.

Remember, people can forgive, but it is truly hard to forget.

Be clear in communicating your thoughts and needs.
No one can read your mind.

Beware of gossip. Even if a word of it were true it serves no
good purpose to push a person who already may be stumbling.

Validate others through paying attention to them.
When you truly pay attention to another person
you are in effect validating every fiber of their being.
How amazing that a gift so invaluable is truly so simple to offer.

Let others know – say it or write it –
just how much you care about them or appreciate them;
whether they are a mechanic who fixed your car or a
friend who got you tickets to a concert.
Don't assume they already know.

Give people feedback. Let them know they matter.
Deserved compliments go a long way.

Remember important dates.

Don't forget you are your sister's and brother's hero.
Be a fan club for them – support them, praise them,
encourage them, honor their individuality.
Remember their birthdays.

HE LOVES ME...
He Loves me NOT...

You don't need a man to complete you,
you need him only to love you.
~ Mom

It's all about love… love is huge.

Really, it's all about loving and being loved. No matter how many things you possess, how many things and people you busy yourself with, one's heart is always in pursuit… of that certain kind of happiness.

Do not rush. Take your time in deciding on "the one!"

First ensure that your relationship is healthy, and then…
just love him. Simply love him.
And allow him to love you back.

The pursuit of happiness in love takes courage.
Sometimes you may have to walk away, take risks, make yourself
vulnerable to hurts, obstacles, criticism, and new challenges…
to in the end be in possession of genuine love is the reward.

The heart has reasons
which the reason cannot understand.
~ Blaise Pascal

There is a cruel truth about romantic love – love is not invincible.
It is like the most delicate of flowers in a prized garden.
You will need to care for it – in the best of times, and in the
worst of times.

When you are deciding on "the one" –
ensure there are no compromises in your heart; in this case
it will not stand the test of time.
Ensure you have no doubts. If doubts come to trouble you,
walk away, even if already at the altar steps.

Invest in yourself and in your future relationships.
If you can, take the time to live alone for at least one year
before you marry.
Surely you deserve at least that much time – and it is so
important – to really get to know yourself, to learn to get
comfortable with yourself, to discover the wonder of you!

Ensuring that you know yourself will ensure that the
person you offer to another is more complete, richer,
dynamic, resilient, confident, decided, and strong…
prepared for all the wonder and promise of love.

Without a question you should know and feel you are
the leading lady in his heart.
Your heart should sing, "He's crazy about me!"

To be treated like a lady? …expect it and allow it!

Choose a boyfriend who lets you be you, loves your
company, but can also stand apart from you,
one you can laugh with and have a ton of fun with.
A sense of humor is more important than
you would ever guess.

Choose a boyfriend you find intellectually stimulating.

If you are contemplating marrying a certain man, be sure
you accept him and love him just the way he is.
You cannot change anything about him,
nor should you want to.
And be absolutely certain that he has no expectations
to change you!

Learn to put your feelings into words.
If not, it is likely that eventually your relationship will fade
into a colorless existence and you will risk that so much of
life will pass you by.

True, some things do not need to be said at all,
but some things will never be heard unless they are told.

Treat your boyfriend, one day your husband, like a prince –
because he is your prince.

Keep the expectations of your relationship real –
one person cannot fulfill everything in you.
That is why we are blessed with friendships.

In your search for love, chances are,
you will experience a broken heart, once or twice.
Trust that it was not meant to be; that time will, yes it will,
heal your broken heart –
and trust that the intended love of your life is waiting for
you just around the corner, somewhere… sometime…
You will survive – with flying colors!
And in the end you will be glad all was as it was.

How will you know if he is "the one?"
I don't know… but when you look at him,
all the power of love will awaken inside you and something
in you will be unchained…
your eyes now open wider, your heart now beating faster,
asking, "just give me your smile!"…
then you will know you are into something good!

Get dressed up once in a while for a 'night on the town'! –
just you and your guy!!!

"Just because!" is the best reason to give a kiss
on the forehead, a tight bear hug, or a flower.

I KNOW YOU KNOW, But...

Believe in Santa!

Stand up straight.

Exercise! Stay fit, look fit, walk fit.

Eat only when you are hungry.

Eat responsibly. It's up to you to take care of your body — it has to last you a long time.

Take care of your skin.

Accept your body – it's perfect for you!

Floss your teeth regularly – they have to last you forever too.

Take the time to take care of yourself – don't "let yourself go!"

Put a napkin on your lap during meals.
Use a knife. Hold your fork properly.
Twirl spaghetti in a spoon.
Don't lick your fingers – use a napkin.

Write your own thank-you notes, promptly.

Shower every day, look clean, smell clean.

Try to keep your room tidy.

Wash your sheets regularly.

Keep up with your laundry.
Sort the darks (cold water), whites (hot water)
and brights (warm water).

Don't walk around wrinkled – iron, or buy wrinkle free.
Take your clothes out of the dryer when they are still warm
and hang or fold them.

Re-vamp your closet once in a while;
give to charity any clothes you haven't worn in the past year.

Don't leave your drink unattended at parties.
Use designated drivers. Stay in control of your body.

Be wise if traveling alone.

Wear a helmet whenever it is recommended.

Return everything you borrow.

Return important phone calls promptly.

Try to shop on sale.

Should you buy that item of clothing?
Only if you can afford it, and if it makes you say, "WOW!",
when you try it on (otherwise, in your closet it sits!).

Dress to please you and not someone else.

Dress as would be appropriate for the occasion.

Remember, fashion fads are in style only if they flatter you!

How you dress and how you behave reflects
more than words can say.
Be respectful of yourself, and others.

KEEP A LITTLE BLACK DRESS IN YOUR CLOSET!!!

Life is either a daring adventure
Or nothing.

~ Helen Keller

IT'S A BEAUTIFUL LIFE!
It's a Beautiful WORLD!

To be in pursuit of our own happiness
we must adequately love ourselves –
only then will this pursuit for us become imperative,
lead us to unquestionable truths,
and transport us to undeniable destinations.
~ Mom

Seize the moments!
Connect with your moods,
connect with your emotions!
Make lists of your own "Top Ten" movies, songs, vacations,
weekend pastimes, books to read…
anything that counts for you!

On these pages, just a few ideas to start your own list:

Happiness is not something ready made...
It comes from your own actions.

~ Dalai Lama

Somewhere, sometime, it may feel like the perfect thing to do! Do it at least once in your lifetime... it's all about ADVENTURE...

1. Live in a foreign country for a year.
2. Hike through a rainforest to the rim of a volcanic crater.
3. Dance outside like no one is watching.
4. Kiss in the rain.
5. Stay in bed all day, order in, read books, your favorite magazines, doodle.
6. On the spur of the moment, take a day off, spend a special day with yourself – turn up the radio and drive to a resort.
7. Volunteer in another country.
8. Give a gift to a stranger.
9. Drop a strawberry into a glass of good champagne, light a ton of candles, listen to your favorite music…
10. Ride the Orient Express!

Love is, above all, the gift of oneself.

~ Jean Anouilh

Get in the car, roll down the windows on a country road, turn up the volume and let your hair fly! Sing about LOVE!

1. Unchained Melody
2. From This Moment On
3. I Will Always Love You
4. The First Time I Ever Saw Your Face
5. Amazed
6. I Don't Want To Miss A Thing
7. All My Life
8. I'll Make Love To You
9. Sugar Sugar
10. My Little Lupa Lu

Escape and become a part of someone else's life for two hours! These movies are SO ROMANTIC!

1. The Notebook
2. Titanic
3. Grease
4. Ghost
5. An Officer And A Gentleman
6. Love Story
7. Pretty Woman
8. West Side Story
9. My Fair Lady
10. Gone With The Wind

What's in a CITY? Go and SEE!

1. Sydney
2. Paris
3. Venice
4. Beijing
5. Amsterdam
6. Prague
7. Buenos Aries
8. Moscow
9. Florence
10. Dubrovnik

Man made WONDERS to let your imagination soar... take it all in...

1. The Taj Mahal
2. Great Wall of China
3. Cologne Cathedral
4. Temple of Abu Simbel
5. Pyramids of the Pharaohs at Giza
6. Temple of Wat Phar Keao
7. Prague and the Charles Bridge
8. The Pillars of Baalbek
9. China's Clay Army
10. Stonehenge

Take in the NATURAL AWES that will
stun your senses...

1. Mount Everest
2. Ngorongoro Crater
3. The Craters of Kilimanjaro
4. The Sahara Desert
5. Great Barrier Reef
6. Iceland's Hot Springs
7. The Iguacu Falls
8. Sequoia National Park
9. Grand Canyon National Park
10. Patagonia

Your time may be limited,
but your imagination is not.

~ Anonymous

Once upon a BOOKSHELF...

1. Anna Karenina
2. Ghandi
3. The Poisonwood Bible
4. The Grapes of Wrath
5. Pillars of the Earth
6. Angela's Ashes
7. A Thousand Splendid Suns
8. Memoirs of a Geisha
9. War and Peace
10. Grimm's Fairytales

Every problem contains the seeds
of it's own solution.

~ Anonymous

Something to seriously THINK about when you watch this movie...

1. Forest Gump
2. Hotel Rwanda
3. Life is Beautiful
4. Schindler's List
5. Welcome to Sarajevo
6. The Devil Came on Horseback
7. An Inconvenient Truth
8. A Beautiful Mind
9. The Color Purple
10. Miracle on 34th Street

You didn't know it, but...

ALL ALONG IT WAS i
WHO WAS LEARNING
IN your CLASSROOM

All my treasures
for the world to see,
all my joys to share with thee,
the love in my heart holds the key,
come play with me.

~ Mom (from Taylor's cart)

One day upon another
my eyes were watching you, loving you, and I have learned…

That children do not belong to parents –
they are only on loan for a fleeting moment,
but one that transforms all time in a lifetime.

That all loves are true loves.

That knowing you is loving you.
That loving you is trusting one's life will count in all things
important, and set ablaze all the promise and goodness of life.

That sometimes the most ordinary things are the
most special things.

That sometimes the most ordinary days are the
most special days.

That all life is sacred. That I learned from you when you
didn't let me squash a spider or a cricket.

That amazing courage can come in small packages,
and heroic acts in quiet moments.
That I learned when you did a reading at the school
assembly, and your voice did not betray the calamity
I knew was inside your tiny body.

That the sound of a child's laughter can fill the chasms of
the deepest canyons.

That the morning crib holding the glee of a child's eyes
could awaken the whole world inside of me.

That there is no truer way to see a miracle than to
witness it through a child's eyes.

That everything is difficult before it is easy –
and yet a child's drive perseveres
from shoelaces to calculus to…

That a child's hug can warm and heal, that it can carry you,
as on angel's wings, for miles and miles. And it has.

That a mother's kiss can heal a scraped knee or a
wounded heart. It really can. And it has.

That I am smart.
So many questions did you ask me,
I didn't know the answers until you asked me.

That every question deserves, and demands, an answer,
no matter how trivial, no matter how many times it has been
asked and answered before.

That feeling proud leads to feeling confident,
which leads to feeling powerful and capable.

That flowers have no color until we truly stop to smell them
and absorb them. You showed me so many new colors.

That the most beautiful bouquets I have received are those
of hand picked flowers, delivered with urgent running steps
across our yard.

That we should pick only the flowers we want to keep.

That there is always something to look forward to tomorrow if
one learns to listen to a child's heart –
many a backyard dig has turned into a newsworthy excavation
in some far away land!

That when we turned over stones – we moved boulders; when
we built sand castles – we captured adventures,
and when we laughed – we etched memories forever.

That for everything we do, everything we see,
the tenth time can feel like the first time – as long as we take
the care to keep our passion for the present alive.

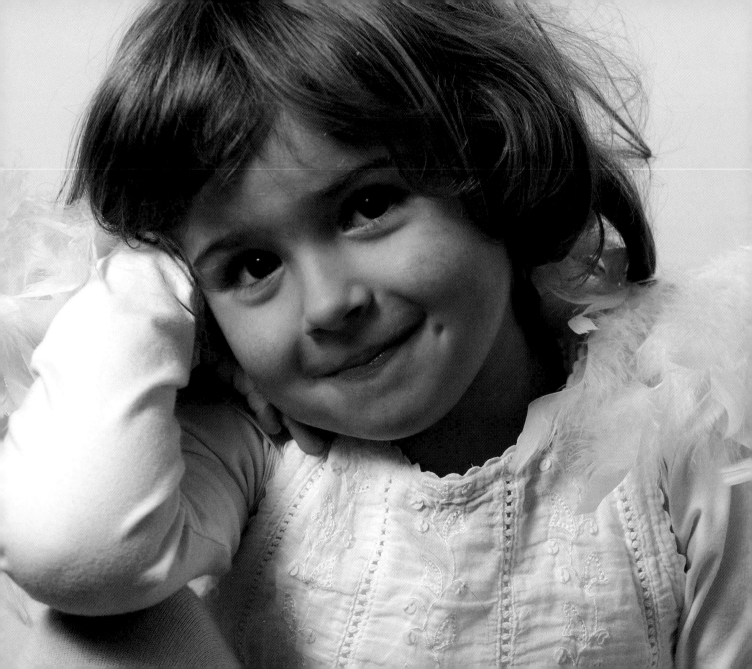

That a child's joy that knows how all those bedtime stories end
is the same joy that knows the sun will rise again tomorrow.

That dreams are sweet when we are able to kiss our child
good night, and even sweeter if we know, that day,
we've given a mother's best.

That your child saying to you, "a job well done,
you passed the grade", would carry so much more value than
any words bestowed by a teacher or employer.

That a revolutionary haircut by a 4 year old child prodigy takes
only a few seconds of 'not watching'!

That peanut butter is good for getting chewing gum out of hair.

That playing dress-up is a dress rehearsal for the greatest fairy tale
ever told, and the heroine is always you!

That when I look back on all the books I have ever read,
you are on all my favorite pages.

That time flies too fast – didn't I just yesterday watch you step
way up to mount the school bus steps?

That more than anyone else, children deserve and require our
attention, respect, and regard. My love you will always have.

Rest assured, my eyes will always be watching you.
Undoubtedly, many more lessons will I learn.
Already you have taken me to the MOON and shown me the STARS!

I love you because… I just do!

ENCORE!

With all it's sham, drudgery, and broken dreams, it is still a beautiful world.
Be cheerful. Strive to be happy.

Max Ehrmann

Always know your family loves you and supports you – no matter what.

Know that our home will always be a place where you can return and hang your heart.

Honor your father and mother.

Cherish your sisters and your brothers.

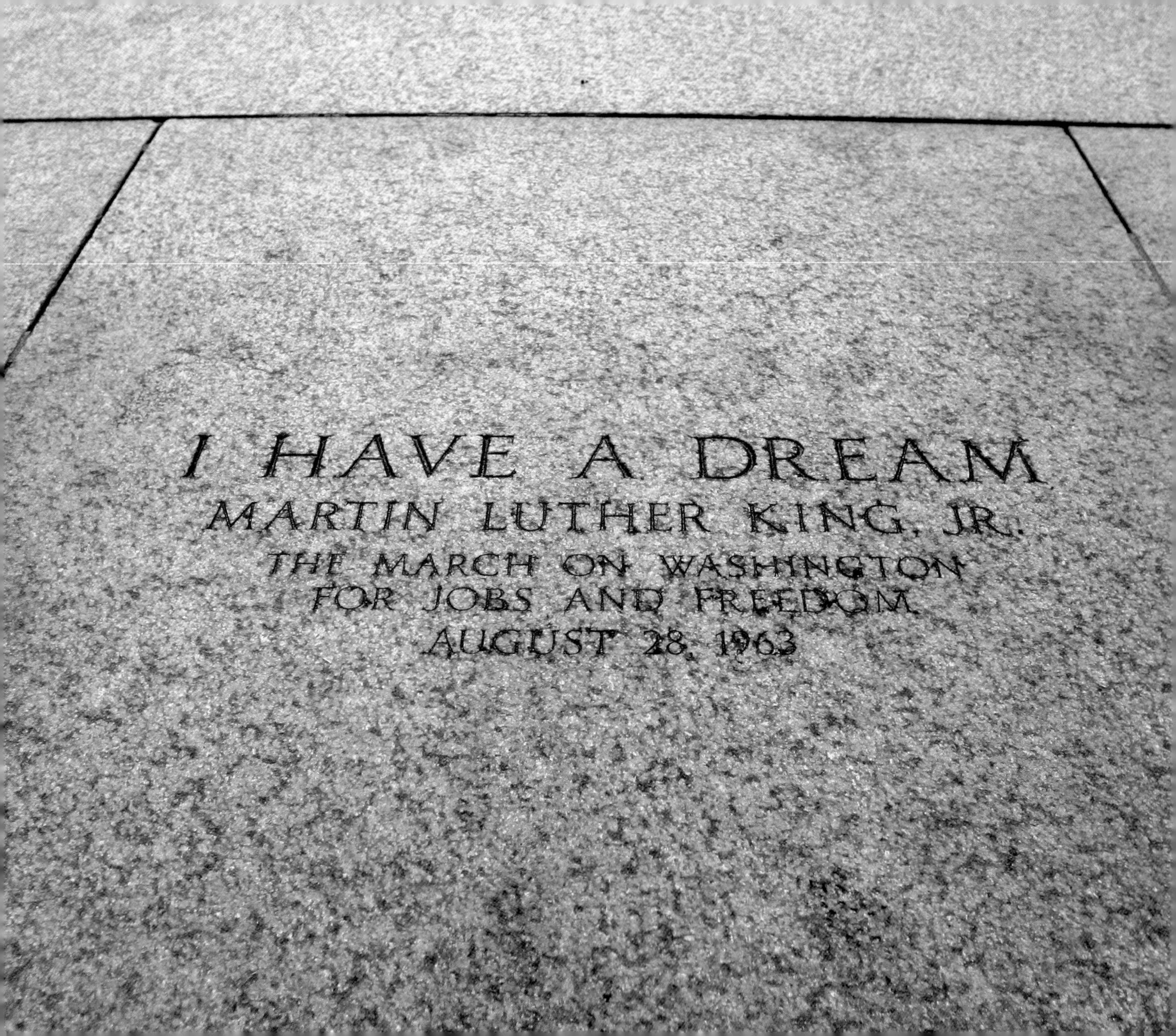

I HAVE A DREAM

MARTIN LUTHER KING, JR.

THE MARCH ON WASHINGTON
FOR JOBS AND FREEDOM
AUGUST 28, 1963

Make a difference.

Be the difference.

Live a noble existence.

Amaze yourself.

Aspire to inspire the best in others.

Celebrate YOU!

It matters.
You matter.
Live a life that matters.

~ *Mom*

Although it was not perfect, I hope my life
was a good enough classroom where you
have heard this all before.

I love you.